A Theatre Royal Plymouth production

AFTER ELECTRA

by April De Angelis

After Electra was first performed on 12 March 2015
at the Theatre Royal Plymouth

Cast

Roy	**Michael Begley**
Shirley	**Rachel Bell**
Virgie	**Marty Cruickshank**
Sonia	**Kate Fahy**
Tom	**Neil McCaul**
Haydn	**Veronica Roberts**
Ori	**James Wallace**
Miranda	**Eleanor Wyld**

Creative Team

Director	**Samuel West**
Set & Costume Designer	**Michael Taylor**
Lighting Designer	**Malcolm Rippeth**
Sound Designer	**Adrienne Quartly**
Casting Director	**Stephen Moore**
Assistant Director	**Phil Bartlett**
Costume Supervisor	**Christopher Cahill**
Consultant Producer	**Jenny Topper**

Production Team

Production Manager	**Nick Soper**
Company Stage Manager	**Paul Deavin**
Deputy Stage Manager	**Christine Grace Hollinshead**
Assistant Stage Manager	**Jennifer Courtenay-Hall**
The Drum Technician	**Matt Hoyle**
Set, props and costumes	**Theatre Royal Plymouth**

with thanks to

Sam Kenyon, Singing Coach
Tom Phillips
Catherine Ring, Drumming Coach
Unicorn Theatre for the use of the drums

Cast Biographies

Michael Begley plays Roy

Theatre credits include: *Mrs Lowry and Son* (Trafalgar Studios), *Sweet Bird of Youth* (The Old Vic), *If There Is I Haven't Found It Yet* (Bush Theatre), *Rhinoceros, The Arsonists* (Royal Court), *Who's Afraid of Virginia Woolf?* (Royal Exchange), *Pravda* (Chichester Festival Theatre and Birmingham REP) and *The Glass Slipper* (Hampstead Theatre). **For television, his work includes:** *Foyle's War, Switch, Doctor Who, Being Human, The Children, William and Mary, City Central* and *Bob and Rose*. **For film:** *Vacuuming Completely in the Nude.*

Rachel Bell plays Sheila

She is a founding member of Hull Truck Theatre Company. **Theatre credits include:** *Keeping Up Appearances* (The Theatre of Comedy), *Alphabetical Order, Pat and Margaret* (Salisbury Playhouse), *Romeo and Juliet* (Stafford Gatehouse Theatre), *Bridget's House* (Hull Truck Tour/Bush Theatre), *The Gladhand, Flying Blind* (Royal Court), Samba (Tricycle Theatre), and *Under Milk Wood* (National Theatre). **Television credits include:** *Mrs Biggs, Eros Unleashed, The Waiting War, Grange Hill, One Foot in the Grave, A Dark Adapted Eye, The Darling Buds of May, Dear John.* **For film:** *From Time to Time, The Edge of Love, The Death of Klinghoffer, Dirty Bomb* and *Sweet William.*

Marty Cruickshank plays Virgie

Theatre credits include: *Exit The King* (Bath Theatre Royal), *Richard II, The Heresy Of Love, Hamlet, Love in a Wood* (RSC), *London Wall* (Finborough/West End), *Pygmalion* (West End/Chichester Festival Theatre), *Gates Of Gold* (Manchester Library Theatre), *In Parenthesis* (Churchill Theatre), *Charley's Aunt* (national tour), *Riders to the Sea, The Tinker's Wedding* (Southwark Playhouse), *Major Barbara* (Piccadilly Theatre). **For television:** *Line of Duty, Spooks, Kavanagh QC, Faith in the Future*, and *Unnatural Pursuits*. **For film:** *London Wall, I, Anna, The Fool.*

Kate Fahy plays Sonia

Theatre credits include: *Definitely the Bahamas* (Orange Tree Theatre), *The Goat* (Almeida/Apollo Theatres), *Grace, Goucho* (Hampstead Theatre), *Old Flames* (Arts Theatre), *Othello* (Young Vic), *Seduced* (Royal Court), and two years at the Everyman Theatre, Liverpool. **Recent television credits include:** *The Meeting of Reason and Squalor, The Suspicions of Mr Whicher*. **Film credits include:** *Archipelago, The Living and the Dead*(for which she received best actress and best supporting actress awards). **As director:** Oliver Cotton's *Wet Weather Cover* (Kings Head, Arts Theatre), Jean-Claude Carriere's *Little Black Book* (Park Theatre).

Neil McCaul plays Tom

Theatre credits include: *Oedipus, Guys and Dolls* (National Theatre), *Romeo and Juliet* (ETT), *Sweeney Todd* (Bristol Old Vic), *Privates on Parade, The Baker's Wife, Chicago, Calendar Girls, A Round Heeled Woman* (West End), *The Boyfriend* (Regent's Park Open Air Theatre), *The Drawer Boy* (Finsborough Theatre). **Television credits include:** *Take Me Home, Into the Fire, Up the Garden Path, Time After Times, Class Act, Where the Heart Is, Crossroads, People Like Us, Benidorm, Father Ted, Heil Honey I'm Home!*

Veronica Roberts returns to Theatre Royal Plymouth to play Haydn

She previously appeared in *Horse Piss for Blood.* **Other theatre work includes:** *Housewife 49* (Old Laundry Theatre), *Nicholas Nickleby* (Chichester, West End, Toronto), *Separate Tables* (Chichester), *Comedy of Errors* (Regent's Park), *Comfort Me with Apples, Buried Alive, Dearly Beloved* (Hampstead Theatre), *Shirley Valentine* (Newbury), *The Glass Menagerie* (Lancaster), *The Shell Seekers* (UK tour), *Being Olivia* (Croydon), *Dancing at Lughnasa (Garrick*). **For television:** *Emma, Party Animals, Afterlife, Little Britain, Tenko, Peak Practice, Playing the Field, New Tricks, Midsomer Murders, Fields of Gold. Playing the Field.* **For film:** *Mr. Turner* (Mike Leigh*), Just Ines, Meet Pursuit Delange.*

James Wallace plays Orin

Theatre credits include: *Blackbeat* (West End/Toronto/Los Angeles), *55 Days* (Hampstead Theatre), *Arcadia, Private Lives* (Manchester Library), *Much Ado About Nothing, Dangerous Corner, Wives as They Were* (Bury St Edmonds), *Volpone, The Duchess of Malfi* (Greenwich), *The Mayor of Zalamea, The Tempest* (Liverpool), *Rosencrantz And Guildenstern Are Dead* (ETT). He has also directed 50 staged readings for Shakespeare's Globe's *Read Not Dead* project. **Film credits include:** *Genius, Piccadilly Jim, Die Another Day.*

Eleanor Wyld returns to Theatre Royal Plymouth to play Miranda

She previously appeared in *The Astronaut's Chair*. **Other theatre credits include:** *Bedroom Farce, Separate Tables* (Salisbury Playhouse), *Visitors* (Arcola Theatre/ national tour/Bush Theatre), *Unscorched, Rigor Mortis* (Finborough Theatre), *Dances of Death* (Gate Theatre), *Antigone* (Southwark Playhouse). **Television credits include:** *Misfits, Black Mirror, Honest, You Can Choose Your Friends.* **For film:** *Bonobo, Johnny English Reborn, Freestyle.*

Creative Team Biographies

April De Angelis | *Writer*

April De Angelis is an acclaimed writer whose extensive theatre work includes *Jumpy* (West End, 2012/Royal Court, 2011); *A Gloriously Mucky Business* (Lyric Hammersmith, 2011); *Calais* (Paines Plough, Oran Mor, 2010) and *Country* (Southwark Playhouse, 2010). April's work for radio includes a serialisation of *Peyton Place*, *Visitants* for BBC Radio 4 and *The Outlander* for Radio 5, which won the 1992 Writer's Guild Award. April has written for Glyndebourne and the English National Opera and wrote *The Silent Twins* libretto, set to music by Errollyn Wallen (Almeida Theatre, 2007). TV work includes a BFI/Channel 4 commission, *Aristophanes*, and she is currently developing a television series with Drama Republic/Channel 4 based on her stage play *Jumpy*.

Samuel West | *Director*

Directing includes: *Close the Coalhouse Door* (Northern Stage, national tour, BBC Radio 4), *Dealer's Choice* (Menier Chocolate Factory/Trafalgar Sudios), *Waste* (Almeida), *Money* (BBC Radio 3), *Così fan Tutte* (ENO) and *The Magic Flute* (Palestine Mozart Festival). As Artistic Director of Sheffield Theatres: *The Romans in Britain*, *Insignificance*, *The Clean House* and *As You Like It* (also RSC). He is an Associate Artist of the Royal Shakespeare Company and Chair of the National Campaign for the Arts.

Michael Taylor | *Designer*

Credits include: *The Ladykillers* (West End, tour, Olivier Award Nomination); *Dead Simple* (UK tour); *Doctor Scroggy's War, Blue Stockings, Anne Boleyn, All's Well That Ends Well, The Winter's Tale, In Extremis* (Shakespeare's Globe); *Eternal Love: The Story of Abelard and Heloise* (ETT UK tour); *Chin Chin* (Bill Kenwright UK tour); *A Little Hotel on the Side* (Theatre Royal Bath); *Sherlock Holmes: The Best Kept Secret* (WYP); *The Misanthrope* (Liverpool); *A Christmas Carol* (Royal & Derngate); *Observe The Sons of Ulster Marching Towards the Somme, Clever Dick, Out in the Open, Keepers, The Awakening, My Boy Jack* (Hampstead Theatre); *Faith Healer; A View from the Bridge, The Price, The Cherry Orchard, The Man Who Had All The Luck, All My Sons, Les Liasons, Dangeruses, Death of a Salesman* (Edinburgh Lyceum); *The Clean House* (UK tour); *Shadow of a Gunman, John Bull's Other Island* (Tricycle Theatre); *Amphibians* (RSC); *Mountain Language* (RNT); *Rafts and Dreams* (Royal Court); *Nova Scotia, The Road to Nirvana* (Traverse); *Darwin in Malibu* (Birmingham Rep); *Winding the Ball* (Royal Exchange); *Private Lives, Present Laughter* (Theatre Royal Bath); *Time and the Conways* (Bristol Old Vic).

Malcolm Rippeth | *Lighting Designer*

Theatre credits include: *The Empress* (RSC); *The Promise* (Donmar); *Spur of The Moment* (Royal Court); *Six Characters in Search of an Author* (Headlong/West End); *The Boy in the Striped Pyjamas* (Chichester); *Calendar Girls* (West End/ Australia/Canada); *Stones in His Pockets* (Tricycle Theatre); *Forever House* (Theatre Royal Plymouth); *Decade* (Headlong); *London* (Paines Plough); *The Dead* (Abbey, Dublin); *The Birthday Party* (Manchester Royal Exchange); *Refugee Boy* (West Yorkshire Playhouse); *His Dark Materials* (Birmingham Rep); *Tutti Frutti* (National Theatre of Scotland); *The Devil Inside Him* (National Theatre Wales); *HMS Pinafore* (Guthrie Theater Minneapolis); *Brief Encounter* (Kneehigh/West End/Broadway; OBIE and WhatsOnStage Awards). **Opera and dance credits include:** *Designer Body* (ballet LORENT); *Orfeo ed Euridice* (Buxton Festival); *Le Nozze di Figaro* (Garsington); *Seven Deadly Sins* (WNO) and *The Coronation of Poppea* (Opera North).

Adrienne Quartley | *Sound Designer*

Sound design credits include: *Merit* (Theatre Royal Plymouth), *Bad Jews* (St James Theatre), *Sex and the Three Day Week* (Liverpool Everyman), *Grand Guignol* (Southwark Playhouse/Theatre Royal Plymouth), *Juvenalia* (Edinburgh Assembly), *Untold Stories* (West Yorkshire Playhouse), *Every Last Trick* (Spymonkey/Royal and Derngate), *A Tale of Two Cities* (Royal and Derngate), *Inside Wagner's Head* (Linbury, Royal Opera House, Theatre Royal Plymouth), *Too Clever By Half* (Manchester Royal Exchange), *Fräuline Julie* (After August) (Barbican Theatre/Schaubühne), *Rings of Saturn* (Halle Kalk, Cologne), *Body of an American* (Gate Theatre), *Get Happy* (Barbican Pit), *Here Lies Mary Spindler* (RSC), *The Container* (Young Vic), *The Shawl* (Young Vic), *Stockholm* (Frantic Assembly/Sydney Theatre Co/Hampstead), *365* (National Theatre of Scotland), *The Roundabout Season* (Paines Plough/Shoreditch Town Hall/Sheffield), *You Can't Take It with You* (Manchester Royal Exchange).

Stephen Moore | *Casting Director*

Theatre credits include: *Merit* (Theatre Royal Plymouth), *Grand Guignol* (Theatre Royal Plymouth/Southwark Playhouse), *Our Boys* (Duchess Theatre), *Ordinary Dreams* (Trafalgar Studios), *Midnight Cowboy* (Assembly Rooms, Edinburgh), *The Exonerated* (Riverside Studios), *Perpetua* (Latchmere Theatre). **Television credits include**: *Father Brown* (BBC), *Watson and Oliver* (BBC), *Very Few Fish* (BBC), *Land Girls* (BBC), *Dawson Bros. Funtime* (BBC), *EastEnders* (BBC), *Doctors* (BBC). **As Casting Assistant:** *Rome* (HBO/BBC), *Longford* (HBO/Channel 4), *The Virgin Queen* (BBC), *He Knew He Was Right* (BBC), *Byron* (BBC). **Film credits include**: *The Contractor.* **As Casting Associate:** *Starter for Ten, Amazing Grace, Brothers of the Head.* **As Casting Assistant:** *Hot Fuzz, The Illusionist, Sahara, The Heart of Me, I Capture the Castle.* **Short films**: *Flea, Chicken Soup, Earthquake, Ela.*

Phil Bartlett | *Assistant Director*

Phil studied English Literature at the University of Oxford and trained as a director at the Royal Conservatoire of Scotland. In 2014 he was a finalist for the JMK Young Director's Award. **Directing credits include:** *The Madness of Lady Bright* (CCA); *The Special* (Traverse, tour); *A Million Hearts in Stereo* (The Arches). **As Assistant Director:** *Merit, Another Place, Grand Guignol* (Theatre Royal Plymouth); *Bite the Bullet* (Òran Mór); *As You Like It* (Bard in the Botanics). Phil is Assistant Director for Theatre Royal Plymouth 2014–2015.

Jenny Topper | *Consultant Producer*

Jenny was Artistic Director of Hampstead Theatre until 2003. During her time there, she produced some 126 plays, 41 of which had a further life in the West End, on Broadway or on tour. Notable transfers to the West End: *A Room Of One's Own* with Eileen Atkins; *Burn This* by Lanford Wilson, with John Malkovich and Juliet Stevenson; *Someone Who'll Watch Over Me* by Frank McGuinness; *Dead Funny* by Terry Johnson; *The Memory of Water* by Shelagh Stephenson; *Little Malcolm and His Struggle Against the Eunuchs* by David Halliwell and with Ewan McGregor; and Mike Leigh's *Abigail's Party*. Prior to this, Jenny was a Director of the Bush Theatre. Having commissioned and opened the new Hampstead Theatre, Jenny continued to produce plays in the West End and on tour including: *The Goat* by Edward Albee with Kate Fahy, Jonathan Price and Eddie Redmayne; the acclaimed production of Albee's *Who's Afraid of Virginia Woolf?*, starring Kathleen Turner; *Martha, Josie and the Chinese Elvis* by Charlotte Jones; *Duet for One* by Tom Kempinski, with Henry Goodman and Juliet Stevenson; *End of the Rainbow* by Peter Quilter (West End, tour and Broadway) *The Three Lions* by William Gaminara; and *Daytona* by Oliver Cotton (Park Theatre, tour, West End). From March 2015 *The Three Lions* will be on tour and at the St. James Theatre, London.

For Theatre Royal Plymouth

Chief Executive	**Adrian Vinken OBE**
Artistic Director	**Simon Stokes**
Executive Producer	**Victoria Allen**
Marketing and Communications Director	**Marianne Locatori**
Operations Director	**Helen Costello**
Theatre Manager	**Jack Mellor**

Board of Directors

Chairman	**Sir Michael Lickiss**
Vice Chair	**Mrs Janie Grace**

Board Members

Mr Nick Buckland, Mr Francis Drake, Ms Bronwen Lacey
Mr Robin Tatam, Mr Peter Vosper, Mr Paul Woods

Theatre Royal Plymouth

Producer

The Theatre Royal Plymouth is the largest and best-attended regional producing theatre in the UK and the leading promoter of theatre in the South West. We produce and present a broad range of theatre in our three distinctive performance spaces – The Lyric, The Drum and The Lab – including classic and contemporary drama, musicals, opera, ballet and dance.

We specialise in the production of new plays and have built a national reputation for the quality and innovation of our programme. Our extensive creative learning work is pioneering and engages young people and communities in Plymouth and beyond. Our award-winning waterfront production and learning centre, TR2, is a unique building with unrivalled set, costume, prop-making and rehearsal facilities.

Recent Theatre Royal Plymouth productions include *Grand Guignol* and *Horse Piss for Blood* by Carl Grose, *Merit* by Alexandra Wood, *Another Place* by DC Moore, *Chekhov in Hell* by Dan Rebellato, *The Astronaut's Chair* by Rona Munro, *Solid Air* by Doug Lucie, and *MAD MAN* by Chris Goode.

The Theatre Royal Plymouth also collaborates with some of the best artists and theatre makers in the UK and beyond. We have regularly co-produced with Paines Plough (*The Angry Brigade* by James Graham, *Love Love Love* by Mike Bartlett), Ontroerend Goed (*Fight Night, Sirens, All That is Wrong*), Frantic Assembly (*Othello*, *The Believers* by Bryony Lavery, *Lovesong* by Abi Morgan) and Told by an Idiot (*My Perfect Mind, And the Horse You Rode In On*)

We have also co-produced with Complicite (*The Master and Margarita, A Disappearing Number*), Hofesh Shechter (*Sun, Political Mother*) and David Pugh, Dafydd Rogers and Kneehigh Theatre (*Rebecca*).

Alongside our own productions we present a programme of quality and popularity and regularly launch national touring productions including *Swan Lake* and Edward *Scissorhands* (Matthew Bourne) and *War Horse* (National Theatre).

After Electra

April De Angelis's plays include *Wild East* (Royal Court), *A Laughing Matter* (Out of Joint/NT/tour), *The Warwickshire Testimony* (RSC), *The Positive Hour* (Out of Joint/Hampstead/Old Vic; Sphinx), *Headstrong* (NT Shell Connections), *Playhouse Creatures* (Sphinx Theatre Company), *Hush* (Royal Court), *Soft Vengeance* (Graeae Theatre Company), *The Life and Times of Fanny Hill* (adapted from the James Cleland novel), *Ironmistress* (ReSisters Theatre Company), *Wuthering Heights* (adapted from Emily Brontë's novel for Birmingham Rep), *Jumpy* (Royal Court and Duke of York's Theatres) and *Gastronauts* (Royal Court). Her work for BBC Radio includes *Visitants*, *The Outlander*, which won the Writers' Guild Award 1992, and *Cash Cows* for the *Woman's Hour* serial. For opera: *Flight* with composer Jonathan Dove (Glyndebourne, 1998), and the libretto for *Silent Twins* (Almeida, 2007).

also by April De Angelis from Faber

APRIL DE ANGELIS: PLAYS 1
(*Ironmistress, Hush, Playhouse Creatures, The Positive Hour*)

A WARWICKSHIRE TESTIMONY

A LAUGHING MATTER

WILD EAST

AMONGST FRIENDS

JUMPY

APRIL DE ANGELIS

After Electra

FABER & FABER

First published in 2015
by Faber and Faber Limited
74–77 Great Russell Street, London WC1B 3DA

Typeset by Country Setting, Kingsdown, Kent CT14 8ES
Printed in England by CPI Group (UK) Ltd, Croydon CR0 4YY

A CIP record for this book
is available from the British Library

ISBN 978–0–571–32615–0

2 4 6 8 10 9 7 5 3 1

After Electra was first performed at the Theatre Royal Plymouth on 12 March 2015. The cast, in alphabetical order, was as follows:

Roy Michael Begley
Shirley Rachel Bell
Virgie Marty Cruickshank
Sonia Kate Fahy
Tom Neil McCaul
Haydn Veronica Roberts
Orin James Wallace
Miranda Eleanor Wyld

Director Samuel West
Set and Costume Designer Michael Taylor
Sound Designer Adrienne Quartly
Lighting Designer Malcolm Rippeth
Casting Director Stephen Moore
Consultant Producer Jenny Topper

Characters

Virgie

Haydn

Tom

Sonia

Shirley

Orin

Roy

Miranda

AFTER ELECTRA

Setting

Virgie's cottage/bungalow on the Essex coast,
opening on a Sunday in September 2014

SCENE ONE	*late morning*
SCENES TWO AND THREE	*after lunch*
SCENE FOUR	*evening*
SCENE FIVE	*October*
SCENE SIX	*April, late morning*
SCENE SEVEN	*late April, early evening*

SCENE ONE

Two women, Virgie (eighty-four years old) and her daughter, Haydn (fifty-eight), stand in the room. Haydn is smoking.

Virgie Would you like the photos?

Haydn Not particularly.

Virgie I'll burn them.

Haydn That's a bit extreme.

Virgie There's nothing sadder than seeing old photos in second-hand shops, gone irreversibly astray. I'm not subjecting Aunt Hilda and Uncle Bill to that. Having them smiling out at nothing.

Haydn So you're going to immolate them?

Virgie Better than having them sniffed at by strangers. Hilda was always so particular about what she wore.

Haydn You might feel differently in a few months, want their company.

Virgie There's something spiritual in consigning them to the flames. I saved everything; my feminist postcard collection: it begins when you sink, in his arms it ends with your arms in his sink. Interested?

Haydn Naturally. I really do have room in my life for all sorts of pointless junk.

Virgie I'll burn that too then.
This is turning out to be marvellously straightforward. What did I think I was saving all this stuff for? Dragging it round for years and years.

How about a dining-room table and four chairs?

Haydn Stop engaging in termination behaviour. It's tasteless.

Virgie Do you want the car?

Haydn For God's sake, you're not dying, are you?

Virgie No.

Haydn Good. Can we get things on a more normal footing. You talk about things that don't interest me and I pretend to listen.
Then I can pop back on to the M25 feeling I've done my duty.

Virgie Visiting me must have been dreadful.

Haydn Not really, I fantasise about the nice glass of cold Chardonnay waiting for me at home.
The bottle chilling in the fridge; gorgeous icy bloom on the green glass.

Virgie What's that, a breast substitute?

Haydn Well, I do qualify. By the way – happy birthday.

Virgie Thank you.

Haydn hands her a parcel. Virgie doesn't open it.

Look, I don't think there's an easy way to tell you this so I'll just give it to you on the chin.
I'm going to kill myself.

Pause.

Haydn Well, that really takes the fucking biscuit.

Virgie Yes, sorry.

Haydn What's brought this on?

Virgie Nothing. I've enjoyed my life. I've had a good innings. I've done everything I wanted to and I'd like to go now before things get any worse. I wasn't looking forward to the decrepit bit. My eyes aren't getting any better. My hands – can't hold a brush. I don't want to go gaga. It's my decision. It's perfectly rational. What I suggest is you accept it and we can get on with having our final day together. The weather's fabulous. Couldn't ask for better in September.

Haydn For God's sake, Mother.

Virgie I want you to stay for the evening. Should be able to let you go by midnight.
  The traffic will be better then. I've invited a few close friends – those I've got left, and I'd like you to help me out –
  I need to prepare a lot of salads –

Haydn Will you listen to yourself.

Virgie holds up her hand.

Virgie I actually managed to cut myself the other day, a knife slipped – 'my thumb instead of an onion'! What a coincidence . . . so that's slowed me down considerably –

Haydn If you think I'm going to preside over some ghoulish scene of self-murder you are absolutely mistaken, I won't do it.

Virgie I'm asking you as a last request and if you say no, Haydn, I'll never speak to you again till the day I die. It may be a short silence but it will be profound, I guarantee.

Haydn If I stay I shall be doing everything in my power to prevent you.

Virgie I didn't expect killing myself would be so demanding.

Haydn You've only just scratched the surface.

Virgie I'm not doing this thoughtlessly. I googled it. 'The intentional, sudden and violent nature of the loved one's death often makes those left behind feel abandoned, helpless and rejected.' That's what I'm trying to avoid.

Haydn How are you going to do it? Dying's messy. Pills get puked up. Jump in front of a train you traumatise the driver. Guns – do you really want other people wiping up your brains? Knives hurt.

Virgie I thought about that. Look.

They look. The sea stretches before them.

I suddenly realised it was out there all the time.

Haydn looks at her mother looking at the sea.

You won't need to bury me. I'm going to be eaten by fish.
I've eaten a lot of fish in my lifetime. I'd like to return the favour.

Haydn That's preposterous.

Virgie I'm not asking you to do anything. I'm just letting you know.
Perhaps you'd like to walk out there with me. Leave me, don't look back.
It only takes a minute to drown. And living here I've often wondered, you know, what it would be like.

Haydn You're depressed. Have you seen Dr Roberts?

Virgie I got old, Haydn. Get over it.

Haydn starts to breathe shallowly. She is having a panic attack.

Have you swallowed a cigarette butt?

Haydn finds it hard to breathe. She begins to stumble about.

You're not dying, are you? Trust you to steal my fire.

Haydn manages to find a paper bag and begins breathing into it. She manages to calm down.

I've managed to live through a whole eighty-four years without seeing a panic attack and now on my last day ever! Well, I wouldn't have missed it. Most people would have cried. But you have an attack. What's that called?

Haydn Conversion hysteria.

She slowly gets to grips with her breathing. Virgie watches her but does not help.

Virgie I didn't open my present!
How exciting.

She opens it. A book.

That's lovely. *Tai Chi for Beginners*. I don't think I'll be able to get through it by midnight. I intend to be intensively socialising. Perhaps you could take it back with you?

Pause.

Whatever.

I'm going to use the last of the lettuce from the garden. It's sublime.

Isn't nature wonderful? It's such a pity we're destroying it. How do you account for that? People are cunts? Shall we start the salads?

Haydn makes no move to help.

You were always so traditional. Let this be the day you make a departure from the predictable. You might discover a whole new you! I'm your mother and I love you. Trust me.

Haydn You're threatening suicide in my presence, I don't think that qualifies as adequate loving care.

Virgie You're fifty-eight, how long was it supposed to go on – this mother thing? Surely there comes a time when my life is my own to dispose of how I please?

Haydn Why couldn't you have just got it over quietly then instead of indulging in this display of theatrics?

Virgie Well, I prefer you being angry with me to all that Victorian panting into a bag.

Haydn I haven't had an attack like that for years.

Virgie I suppose it's all my fault.

Haydn Frankly yes.

Virgie If you feel so badly about it perhaps you'd better go.

Haydn I can't go, Mother, because I'd feel guilty for the rest of my life – what would have happened if I'd stayed, I could have prevented you, etc., etc. I'm trapped unless I can think of a way out. Ooh, maybe I'll kill myself. Except I'm not a coward.

Virgie I'm not a coward, Haydn. I'm quite scared of water.

Haydn I know what this is about. You're frightened of getting sick and being on your own. I would have visited.

Virgie You know nothing.

Haydn You've got everything to live for.

Virgie What have I got to live for? You don't like me, never have really, you've tolerated me and I've loved you of course because being a mother is like being a madwoman, you're visited by a kind of insane, boundless love for your children that has no known precedent.

Haydn Is that why you left me with Bill and Hilda?

Virgie Summer in the countryside – wonderful.

Haydn You abandoned me there.

Virgie I visited –

Haydn For two years.

Virgie Was it as long as that? Farmhouse Christmases, lovely.

Haydn I cried myself to sleep.

Virgie I expressed my love in trying to change the world. Painting, that was my way, that was for you.

Haydn Thank you very much – I was a child, I didn't appreciate it.

Virgie It seemed selfish to you but I was surviving, spiritually. I used to meet a lot of dead women at the shops.
Housewives. They only appeared living if you weren't looking closely. This is a trip down memory lane.

Haydn You did the best you were capable of but kids need a secure routine.

Virgie Don't remind me. The tedium. Not your fault. You were children, you couldn't help making the same wretched endless demands.

She sees something out of the window.

Oh look, here are the first guests.
This is what the Romans did – have a feast and then fall on their swords. It's civilised.

Haydn I'm just warning you I will be doing all in my power to disrupt –

Virgie You think you mind now, Haydn, but I assure you really you'll be pleased. You've never liked me and you can inherit the cottage. And there are a few paintings. You'll have to forgive me and help out. It'll be cathartic.

Enter a couple, Tom, sixty-eight, still handsome, and Sonia.

Tom Virgie!

They embrace.

Sonia Virgie, love.

Virgie Hello Tom, hello Sonia.

Tom Happy birthday to you, but it is impossible – birthdays are wasted on you. You are immortal, ageless –

Virgie You're flattering me. You remember Haydn – my daughter.

Tom Little Haydn, hello.

Sonia Hello.

Tom This is good, isn't it?
Wonderful. We love it here.

Sonia It's so pretty. And the light's so good for your painting.

Virgie Delightful, isn't it?

Tom You haven't changed, Virgie. Age cannot wither her.

Sonia Tom's declaiming. He's been at the RSC.

Virgie Good for Tom.

Haydn Virgie's got a surprise.

Tom God, I hate surprises.

Haydn You've come to the right place then.

Sonia Look at us – we've got your present in the car. The manuscript of my new book – you did say you wanted to read it? And some champagne.

Tom Six for five. You're not eighty-four every day.

Virgie I shan't be drinking.

Tom I've heard that before.

Virgie I don't want to die drunk.

Sonia We're not suggesting you drink the whole lot alone and at once.

Tom Although it would be a laugh – we could help. Virgie's always been very good value with a few beers down her.

Virgie Yes, but I want to be stone cold sober when I commit suicide. I don't want anything going wrong. I don't want to be doing it all over again on Monday morning.

Pause.

Tom I suggest we crack a bottle open now.

Sonia Tom – don't you think we should react to what Virgie just said?

Tom I didn't understand of word of what she just said, it didn't make sense.

Sonia How do you survive as a bloody actor? Too busy thinking about what you're going to say next, never listening. She said – perhaps you could help me out here, Haydn, she said – is that what she said?

Tom We just want to clarify what you meant, Virgie, when you said . . . what you said.

Haydn My mother is going into the sea and she's not coming back.

Tom Are you swimming to France?

Sonia She's eighty-four.

Haydn She's not planning to get that far.

Tom You mean you are . . . swimming . . . and swimming and not returning –

Virgie Yes. I don't think swimming is the right word. I'll be sitting at the confluence of tides. I just want to say goodbye properly. You mustn't think of death in a grim way, it's just a change from one form of existence to another.

Tom From warm, passionate, sensate life –

Sonia I hope you're not describing yourself.

Tom – to a lump of dead meat.

Sonia That's more like it.

Tom Christ, Sonia, is it going to be like this all day? We've only just arrived.

Sonia Virgie could you confirm that you are going to –

Virgie Yes.

Sonia Oh God.

Tom What nonsense.

Pause.

What a bloody awful thing to do.

Haydn Yes.

Virgie I want today to be a celebration.

Tom My God my God my God my God my God.

Virgie With the people that mean something to me. Would you like a drink? A gin and tonic, some wine?

Tom My God.

Virgie Or a soft drink or a cup of tea – you have been travelling?

Tom It's not possible I can't believe it this is terrible news I'm coming with you.

Virgie No no no.

Tom Yes.

Sonia Don't be a prat, Tom.

Virgie This is my exit.

Tom A light will go out.

Virgie I know what I'm doing.

Tom What about Haydn?

Virgie What about her?

Tom You're her mother.

Virgie I am also a person in my own right.
Well, I'm glad we've got that out of the way.

Shirley enters.

Shirley Hello, hello, everyone, It's me! I come to shower my sister with gifts.

She kisses everyone.

When does the fun start?

Tom We're all feeling a little put out, Shirley, because Virgie's decided she's going to kill herself.

Shirley I don't think so.

Virgie Yes, I've got the order of events.

Tom That's a bit morbid.

Virgie Death is morbid. Tom?

Tom takes it.

Tom Order of Events. We have free time till drinks before lunch. There are a range of available snacks including a vegan alternative.

An optional stroll on the beach.
Lunch at one-thirty.
Followed by an address by each one of us to Virgie or if we prefer an entertainment of some sort.
Virgie addresses us.
After dinner we have the lighting of *the bonfire*.
Then we go home and Virgie tops herself. She's underlined it, look. She's gone mad.

Sonia Do you really think we're going to sit by and let you do it, Virgie?

Virgie You're my oldest friends, I expect you to respect my wishes.

Shirley Someone get me a sherry for Christ's sake.

Virgie Dry or medium?

Shirley I don't fucking care at this juncture. Who can tell the difference after two glasses?

Virgie You're not supposed to have two glasses, it's an aperitif.

Shirley Are these people living in the real world? Now I want you to stop all this nonsense and let everyone breathe a sigh of relief and then we can all have a jolly time.

Virgie Go away, Tom and Sonia, go for a walk while I do the family thing.

Sonia Talk some sense into her.

Tom You should have told us what you were up to, Virgie, We're not wearing the right clothes. This light jacket . . .

Sonia He doesn't feel dressed for the part.

Shirley Leave it to me.

Tom and Sonia exit.

They're hard work. Well, I came. Husband said to me these things have to be done, these big occasions have to be marked.

Virgie How is James?

Shirley Excellent. Retirement bores the arse off him.

Virgie And how's life as a Lord?

Shirley Well, it's what I was born for but I don't think we should get on to that side of things do you?

Virgie I'm not afraid.

Shirley Of the hurly-burly? No, neither am I. Virgie, I've been looking forward to today – to be embraced in the bosom of my family and its banal everyday life – and you have to go and pull a stunt like this. Cancel it, will you? Happy birthday.

She hands her an envelope.

Virgie What is it?

Shirley It's a holiday in Venice.

Virgie I won't be going.

Shirley Don't be silly. It's a Renaissance jewel – you want to see it again before it goes underwater.

Virgie Well, it's very kind but I won't be in a fit state to travel. I'll be underwater myself before then.

Shirley Oh come on, stop it, it's me, Shirley – stop posturing. I love you, Virgie and we're sisters. Now is a special time in our lives when we can sit back and mull over our achievements. I'm proud of what I've achieved in education.

Virgie Made school more like a factory, you mean?

Squashing all those young minds through the mincer of educational excellence. Ghastly.

Shirley I know we haven't seen eye to eye over the years.

Virgie 'Ofsted' – didn't the parallel with Orwell ever strike you?

Shirley I'm not going to argue, it's your birthday.

Virgie I'm a big enough person to be happy that you want to carry on for whatever reason – but I don't.

She hands Shirley a sherry.

Shirley Don't think I can't see what you're doing. You've always been nasty and spiteful and now you're belittling my life in this revolting way.

Virgie Sorry.

Shirley You're not a bit sorry – you've got the upper hand for once and you're revelling in it. Well, what a pathetic way to achieve power over another individual.

Virgie And you'd know nothing about that of course – headmistress?

Shirley I want your word that you'll drop this.

Virgie No.

Shirley Or we'll have to have you sectioned. (*To Haydn.*) Won't we?

Virgie Is that a threat –

Shirley Of course. It's always something with you, Virgie. Do you remember, Haydn, the naked protest?

Haydn Yes.

Shirley When they spelled the word 'peace' on Foulness. Virgie was the exclamation mark.

That was bloody embarrassing. I was entering the Upper House and my seventy-nine-year-old sister was flashing her bush for demilitarisation.

Haydn That's her right, after all.

Shirley But it's all part of the same thing. A deliberate attempt to unsettle. Like this – now.

Virgie I don't want to argue with you, Shirley life's too short, especially mine.

Shirley I refuse to let you blame me in some way.

Virgie You're just going to have to accept that you're just not important enough to take the blame for this. Sorry.

Pause.

Shirley James and I have been very happy.

Virgie Good for you.

Shirley I'm sorry you never had that.

Virgie I've had plenty of lovers, quite a few of them knew what they were doing and if they didn't I showed them the ropes. So don't be sorry on my account.

Shirley No need to boast. I'm sure that wasn't easy on Haydn. Or Orin.

James and I often talk about what happened. It was a tragedy.

Haydn It was a long time ago and I've had a lot of therapy.

Shirley That's not cheap. Please tell me this is some ridiculous joke, Virgie.

Virgie No, cheers though. Raise a glass to me.

Shirley No. Can't you see, Virgie, when you act in a selfish way there's always casualties. Look at Haydn.

Haydn Thank you.

Shirley Don't take this personally, dear, but you didn't fulfil your potential. I'd like to see you in red.

Virgie Oh, leave her alone, Shirley. Haydn is Haydn, she's all right.

Haydn How would you know? You never ask.

Virgie The surprising thing is I thought seeing you all might make me change my mind, or at least waver a bit. But it's the opposite. I'm actually looking forward to going. Excuse me – I've a guacamole to whisk.

She exits. Tom and Sonia re-enter.

Sonia Raised voices?

Tom It's really happening, then?

Shirley Apparently.

Sonia We can't let it happen.

Shirley Of course not. We might be implicated.

Tom I can't go to prison at my age. One awkward encounter in a shower I'd be dead meat.

Sonia No one's going to bugger you Tom, you're sixty-eight.

Tom God, getting old's depressing.

Shirley I assumed you were straight.

Sonia Primarily he's a narcissist.

Tom Yes, what am I doing moralising to Virgie? I'm an ethical foetus.
Where is she?

Haydn Making the salads.

Shirley What's brought it on?

Sonia We saw her last month – she seemed perfectly fine.

Tom Although it was in a theatre bar. Who's going to say anything meaningful in the interval of *Shrek*?

Sonia People do say interesting things. I often eavesdrop rather than stand there listening to you.

Tom There's usually a general sense of relief to have got halfway without wanting to slit your throat. Sorry, Haydn – theatre hasn't been political since the late seventies. When we ran our theatre collective its ambition was to overthrow the state.

Sonia Then the state stopped funding you.

Tom Growing old is growing disillusioned. Do you think that's why, Virgie?

And to think I was actually looking forward to today. Virgie makes such a delicious quiche. Few glasses of bubbles. Now we've got Hedda bloody Gabler. What do you do, Haydn?

Haydn I'm a bereavement counsellor.

Sonia You knew that, Tom.

Tom This must be a kind of busman's holiday for you, Haydn?

Sonia Sorry, Haydn, this is all very tasteless. Stop being a prick, Tom.

Shirley Has there been some particular trigger – is that the word?

Sonia I expect it's got a lot to do with being a woman.

Women go mad – look at Abigail.

Tom Abigail's not a good example.

Sonia Why?

Tom She is mad. Trying to pretend she's forty-five –

twenty-five even – it's scary. Somebody should have told her that an Alice band is not fooling anyone. She's a crone.

Sonia There's a special brand of contempt reserved for women who get old.

Tom Burning at the stake?

Sonia Oh fuck off, Tom.

Shirley Let's try to put our differences aside for Haydn's sake – for Virgie's sake – let's try and sort this out.

Tom Yes. If she sees us arguing she'll only be confirmed in her desire to kill herself – I know how she feels. Let's encourage her through our practice to re-embrace life.

Shirley That's a good idea.

Sonia How are we going to do that?

Tom Fuck knows, but we'll have to try and imagine what it would be like to be enamoured of life again – it's like a sort of theatre game when you remember when you were happiest. We can try that for an evening and if it doesn't work phone the police.

Shirley Fantastic.

Tom We need to do something – to tempt her with – just to get her over this hiccup.

Sonia You can't describe death as a hiccup – it's like one final God almighty belch.

Tom What's this suicide thing all about Haydn? From a professional point of view?

Haydn Anger towards others turned in on the self.

Shirley I'll never understand that. I'd always prefer to take everything out on my husband, that's what long-term partnerships are for.

Haydn In Virgie's case it could be revenge.

Shirley Revenge? For what?

Sonia She lost a child, that's hard.

Tom Sonia trained as a counsellor.

Sonia Only up to intermediate.

Haydn Life hasn't turned out the way she wanted it. It's a way of punishing us all.

Sonia Why would she want to do that?

Haydn I don't know – I'm not her therapist, just her daughter.

Shirley Well, we can't let her do that. It's preposterous.

Virgie re-enters.

Virgie Is everyone having as much fun as possible under the circumstances?
After lunch we'll take a walk along the beach – lovely, such soft blues, sublime in the garden, edges of the leaves all hazy in the sun.

Tom Oh God, Virgie.

Virgie You worry too much, Tom, it's all going to be fine. Trust me. Why are we all so hung up about death? Look, you all flinched when I said that. Death. Death.
Come and eat.

She exits. They follow.

SCENE TWO

After lunch.

Tom I was surprised how much I managed to force down, in the circumstances.

Sonia Your appetite was so healthy it was positively obscene.

Tom Virgie hates waste. Perhaps we should've phoned the police. I don't like to, though, on her birthday. Also I was looking forward to the pudding.

Shirley It's messy. We should try to sort this out ourselves.

Tom It's pagan, in a way. What Virgie's up to, a ritual.

Sonia You're not in *King Lear* now, Tom. This is Essex.

Tom That could have been Essex. Bloody novelists don't know a thing about the theatre – snobs – and then they think I'll take a break from proper writing and knock out the odd play – and it's really –

Sonia Stop going on.

Tom – really, really, really shit because . . .

Sonia Sorry, Shirley.

Tom Novels are easy compared to plays. Like taking a crap as opposed to building a matchstick Taj Mahal.

Sonia I'm a novelist. Well, I had one published once. I've done a lot of jobs.

Tom Our whole society is drowning in mediocre literature, that's why we're intellectual pygmies.
'The Lemon Drizzle Cake Club.' That's supposed to be a title – I'd rather have my eyes torn out and stuffed up my –

Sonia I'll do that for you if you like.

Shirley Your plan, Tom, of us all being happy is definitely the right way to go.

Virgie enters with Haydn. They carry presents.

Virgie Farewell gifts.

Shirley laughs.

What are you laughing for, Shirley?

Shirley I'm just happy.

She laughs again.

I'm just thinking how nice it is to be together after that lovely meal you made us, Virgie.

Virgie Haydn's been following me around like a lost chick. That's for you.

Gives Shirley a gift.

Shirley Oh, what have I got? Oh, fabulous. What is it? (*Binoculars.*) Am I doing it right?

Everything looks smaller. I like a smaller world! No, it's the other way. These are fantastic. What are they actually for?

Virgie Bird-watching. There's a wider world out there, Shirley, than the corridors of power.

Shirley Don't get a lot of birds in Westminster.

Sonia Pigeons.

Tom No one wants to see a pigeon close up, a lot of them have foot rot. I want to vomit when I see a pigeon.

Virgie For when you retire. You can take up bird-watching as a hobby.

Shirley I won't be retiring for a very very long time.

Virgie You're seventy-six.

Shirley laughs.

I mean how much longer do you plan to go on?

Shirley I'm a lord. Well, I've not given enough time to birds. So thank you. Birds, here I come.
Eventually.

She laughs.

Virgie Laughing doesn't suit you.

Shirley stops laughiing.

Tom When I see a particularly tatty-looking pigeon, gnarled feet, gummy beak, I think, Christ, that'll be me in a few years.

Sonia They have beady eyes like you.

Virgie Sonia!

Sonia I hope this isn't ridiculously generous?

Virgie Really it isn't.

Shirley Mine wasn't. (*Pause.*) It was thoughtful.

Virgie We've moved on from birds, Shirley, get over it.
Why don't you open yours at the same time, Tom? Then we can speed things up a bit.

Tom I don't want to 'speed things up', not if it means –

Virgie Tom.

Tom Won't it be stealing Sonia's fire?

Sonia You don't usually mind.

Virgie Tom!

They open simultaneously.

Sonia O, Virgie, it's beautiful.

She has a painting.

Shirley What is it?

Sonia It's here I think, the sea.

Shirley Every time you look at that you can remember today. Not Virgie killing herself.

She laughs.

Sonia Isn't that sublime, Tom love?

Tom Yes, dearest.

Sonia Thank you, I'll treasure it.

Tom This is too.

He holds a book.

Generous.

Virgie I won't be doing a lot of reading where I'm going.

Shirley A book.

Tom Plays.

Sonia Oh. Lovely.

Tom First edition, *Oresteia.*

Shirley That must be bloody ancient.

Tom Nineteen thirty-six, Louis MacNeice translation.

Shirley Yes, of course. Losing my –

Tom No one has ever given me anything quite so wonderful.

Sonia We've only been married thirty years.
Are you going to say anything else, Tom?

Virgie He's absorbing his gift.

Shirley Your turn, Haydn.

Virgie Haydn hasn't got one.

Haydn It's all right.

Virgie She's going to get everything, she doesn't need a present. My paintings. My life's work.

Haydn Yes, I look forward to that. Don't make a fuss – anyone.

Virgie If you want there's that bead dress I showed you.

Shirley A bead dress – how smashing. What's a bead dress?

Sonia Covered in beads sewn together.

Shirley Why don't you have that? That sounds super.

Haydn Bit like wearing an abacus.

Tom I still can't speak.

Sonia That won't last.

Tom I always wanted to play Clytemnestra.

Sonia Another colour to add to my husband's palette: cross-dresser.

Tom Best part in it.

Haydn Wasn't she a whore?

Tom Murdered by her kids. The Greeks weren't frightened to give the family a bad name.
Thank you, Virgie.

Virgie Finished? Now, I'm offering you the chance to say anything that's been eating at you, there's no point waking up tomorrow morning and thinking, I wish I'd said this or that. I'd always meant to mention to Virgie . . . Now is your chance. I'll be dead tomorrow.

Pause.

No? It could be something big. 'Meeting you was like having an orgasm in the Trevi Fountain as the LSO plays Abba's greatest hits.' Or something more mundane – 'Where do you keep your cheese-grater?'

Shirley I remember that time you made me eat snow. I was seven. They ate snow in Minnesota, you said, with syrup, you'd read it in *Little House on the Prairie*. So I ate it and was sick.

Virgie Thank you, Shirley. Anyone else?

Tom You were the most amazing landlady. You had a little pot with the word 'marijuana' on it and the first thing you said was 'help yourself'. Fantastic. I grew up in a semi in Scunthorpe.

Pause. Sonia indicates she does not want to speak.

Virgie Thank you everybody for that rich and complex portrait. Let's move swiftly on to the entertainments.

Shirley What entertainments?

Tom Traditional birthday ritual customised for suicide party.

Sonia I was going to . . . read this for your eighty-fourth – but here goes.

She reads the first stanza of Jenny Joseph's poem, 'Warning'. Pauses.

Shirley You can do it.

Tom Come on old girl, the last fence.

Sonia continues reading to the end of the poem.

Virgie Thank you.

Tom Well done, love.

Sonia Change your mind, Virgie.

Virgie It's a nice poem but a sentimental middle-class fiction. Eccentric older women do not get rewarded, they get pilloried.

Sonia Ah.

Shirley I haven't a fucking clue what to do. If I'm honest.

Sonia Join in Tom's song.

Tom I'm not sure it's suitable in the circumstances.

Virgie Just do it. We don't want to sit here being gloomy.

Tom Virgie's a hard woman to turn down.

Sonia (*to Shirley*) Just hum along.

Tom sings a version of Nina Simone's 'Ain't Got No Life'.
Virgie joins the last refrain.

Virgie Perfect. Wonderful. I shall hum that as I die.

Haydn Tricky when you're taking on water.

Shirley Absolutely fantastic. Well done, everybody.
Now stop this bloody nonsense, Virginia, or we'll have you sectioned.

Virgie It's my body.
Have you got anything to say, Haydn?

Haydn You'd like us to stop you, there's a frightened part inside you hoping you won't let the more despairing, depressed part of you drive you to do what you don't really want to.

Virgie But apart from all that is there anything you'd like to say to me?
Because I realise you're going to look back on today and wish it had gone a hundred other ways.

Haydn Maybe that's what you're wishing now.

Virgie No.

Haydn You're making a mistake. Suicide – it's impossible to do it in a rational frame of mind – and if you're not rational then you're sick, depressed and you need help.

Virgie What's rational about people? Three-quarters of the planet believe in a supernatural being who is watching over them and is responsible in some way for all this? Don't think I'm unhappy. I'm not. I just want out. I've lived a long time and I just – want – out –

And I'm doing it in a lovely, celebratory way. Like being at my own funeral. I've been actually looking forward to hearing what people had to say about me. I haven't been looking forward to anything so much for ages. Since I've decided to exit in this way I've been really enjoying myself. The mornings are so beautiful. Each new day is so fresh and I hadn't felt that – since I was a child – or painting – I like that feeling of now. It's just greed that makes us want more and more. We're all a bit greedy and spoilt in these rich countries. Well, that's what I've been having these last months and really, Haydn, I can't go back to before – and I won't. Which is why – yes, why I'm going to do it.

Haydn You asked me here so I would stop you.

Virgie Poor Haydn. Do you want a cuddle?

Haydn Between us we can make sure you're safe and won't do anything.

Virgie I refuse to be drugged up to the eyeballs and locked up with men who think they're Jesus.

Shirley The thing is, Virgie, I've got one tit.

Virgie Your point is?

Shirley If I can go around with one tit you can put up with feeling a bit old.

Virgie I don't really see that.

Shirley I don't want you to do this, Virgie, because it's like you're saying to us life's not worth it. Our lives aren't.

Virgie That's your business. You've all got to learn to let people go, to stop being so childish. If I'd imagined this level of immaturity I would never have invited you in the first place. I'd have had a gin and tonic and set off. What, you think life goes on for ever? You can't imagine a worse death? A worse life? This is a world where children go to bed hungry. Get upset about that if you want. Don't be such emotional philistines. Grow up.

Tom Yes, but we like you such a lot.

Sonia I always imagine I can come here to you, Virgie, and be happy, if things get too bad with Tom.

Virgie They are bloody awful with Tom, Sonia. Be happy for me. I've been 'in the present', carefree, since I made my decision.

Tom We aren't so carefree, as it happens, Virgie. We're shitting ourselves.

Virgie Let's just be together, now. Who knows, the world might end in five minutes.

Tom It won't though, will it? That would have been too much of a coincidence.

A voice echoes through the house.

Man's Voice Hello.

Shirley Are we expecting any more guests?

A man enters, this is Virgie's fifty-two- year-old son, Orin. Virgie is not expecting him.

Orin Hello, Mum.

SCENE THREE

Moments later. Virgie, Orin, Haydn.

Virgie I expect you're wondering why I didn't invite you?

Orin To your own funeral? Just a bit.

Virgie I've written you a letter. It's somewhere – I would have asked you but I only have four chairs.

Orin I'm your son.

Virgie I guessed you'd kick up a fuss if you were here.

Orin You guessed right.

Virgie (*to Haydn*) Did you ask him?

Orin Can't I visit my own ma? On her birthday? I need to fill you in. Apparently I haven't got much time.

Virgie Let's do it then. How are the girls?

Orin Jennifer's doing her GCSEs. Dawn's doing a lot of swimming.

Virgie Where does she get that from? And how's Berenice?

Orin Pretty fucked off with my drinking and recidivist level of unemployment. The trouble with being a freelance illustrator – more free than illustrator. Berenice kicked me out. I've been sleeping – in stations.

Virgie She's had you back before.

Orin I wish I shared your buoyancy about the future.

Virgie There are the children.

Orin No guarantee of marital longevity.

Virgie You smell – you could do with a bath.

Orin I've come home.

Virgie It's not a good time.

Orin I've come home. I can't . . . any more . . . Something in me . . . is broken.

Virgie Since when?

Orin I don't know when – it's been building up . . . A kind of . . . everything in me pushing me to –

Virgie This sounds like a big conversation. There are people here – and I've got a schedule.

Orin I had to come home. Like a lost child in a fairy tale wandering the woods looking for something familiar – an old stone they'd cast away – breadcrumbs – a lighted window. Home, I think that's here.

Virgie I might have liked a visit months ago, but now the time for all that is over.

Perhaps you could talk to Haydn about it after I die. She is a bereavement counsellor.

Orin That's harsh.

Virgie Well, it suits her, she has a depressive nature.

Haydn My friends find me quite amusing.

Orin The thing is, Mum, you can't do this to us.

Virgie I can't talk now, I'm busy. Tell him. Haydn, I've got other things on my mind.

Haydn Dying is a kind of accounting for – it's inevitable.

Orin Of all the relationships in the world – mother and child – should be the one you can count on – template for all the others – if that one doesn't work – well, the rest are pretty fucked.

Virgie Life did get a bit chaotic.

Orin I have to pinch myself sometimes to believe we got taken away. That actually happened to me.

Virgie You're a big boy now, Orin. In fact, you've got bigger since the last time I saw you.

Orin Are you saying I've put on weight? Are those going to be your last words to me?

Virgie I want to go now, I'm ready. Let me go.

Orin You don't know what it is to be a mother. Do you?

Virgie When I met your father I thought I liked him but I made a mistake. So I left. Then I began to discover something about myself. My paintings started to get very big.

I was quite frightened of them at first – colour too, as if I'd been starved, lots of reds and one, Mars red, like blood that's dried – you know how it stiffens the material it's caked on – peculiar. I didn't want to live the kind of lives most women did. They bored me. Sorry about that. If I'd been stupider I would have made a better mother.

Orin But if you think about it – now's your chance to make it up. I could stay here with you. And Dawn and Jennifer could come at the weekends and we could do stuff with them. Take them swimming. Dawn's crawl is something to behold. I usually take sandwiches because we'd be in there for the long haul.

Virgie I know one shouldn't make jokes at a time like this but really I'd rather be dead.

Orin No. We won't let you do it.

Virgie What are you going to do? Keep me prisoner?

Haydn You're not leaving us a choice. We'll keep a watch on her. We'll take turns.

SCENE FOUR

Evening. Haydn comes in.

Tom Nowhere?

Haydn Nowhere, nowhere.

Tom So sorry. Do you think she got to the water?

Haydn He fell asleep. I should have smelt the booze on his breath.

Tom Ah yes. Well, when you're in the middle of things it's very hard to change them. You always look back and imagine it's easy but really you're a streetcar stuck on its rails and there's this momentum rushing you forwards and you only have time to stop yourself derailing – re-routing's impossible. That's life.

Sonia has entered.

Sonia This isn't the time for one of your speeches Tom. We should be searching for Virgie.

Tom I think possibly it's too late for that.

Sonia For all we know she could be next door, trapped in a wardrobe.

Tom This isn't fucking Narnia. Virgie has drowned herself. Like she said she would.
She's a woman of her word.

Sonia She wouldn't do that without speaking to me first.

Tom Well, hey ho. She has.

Sonia The sea's bloody freezing this time of year, there's no way she was going in.

Tom She went in. She's incredibly brave. I'd do it if I had half her guts.

Sonia God, you do talk rubbish.

Tom Anyone would think you thought I talked rubbish.

Sonia I don't know why anyone ever bothers to listen to actors? Like they know anything? They haven't actually lived their lives, they've lived other people's. They don't have experiences like us, they have a CV of parts played. Time spent saying words written for them by people who are cleverer than them and have a conscience –

Tom Why don't you have another drink, Sonia? You're not quite marmalised.

Sonia A conscience, a morality, a sense of the world cohering into an idea more expansive than their own stomach, face and cock.

Tom There's a dead woman out there – no one wants to talk about my cock.

Sonia Sure about that, Tom? You are in the room.

She thinks this is funny.

I love being old – you get to be rude and no one tells you to fuck off.

Tom If we could get a word in edgewise, I'm sure we would. Writers on the other hand –

Sonia Old record . . .

Tom Well, I say writers – that usually presumes one has to have written something quite good.

Sonia I've taught creative writing for twenty-five years.

Tom Writing the same novel in endless variation, with decreasing returns.

Sonia I have an award, Haydn. That's how I met your mother – she came to my book-signing.

Tom By accident – she thought it was Sainsbury's.

Sonia You don't hurt me, Tom, because I don't value your opinion.

Tom The same wounded females teetering between despair and empowerment, but they find self-fulfilment in map restoration.

Sonia Tom plays a variety of beards now. Old-blokes-in-beards parts – you never bother to remember the names. Cuntsman the Duke of Cardiff, short and tufty beard. Arsewipe the Earl of Puff, long flowing beard dipped in wee.

Tom Some people do remember the names, Sonia. Those people are clever and take care.

Sonia When Virgie walks back in here I will be laughing.

Pause.

I will.

Tom This is how we get by, Haydn, hating each other.

They all stop as Orin comes back in carrying Virgie, who appears dead, followed by Shirley.

Orin I found her by the side of the path that heads out for the sea. She was in the dark, lying there in the dark.

Shirley I can't get a bloody signal. Where's the phone?

Sonia Oh Virgie.

SCENE FIVE

A month later.

Virgie sits in chair, immobilised. A fold-up wheelchair and a stick are apparent.

Haydn arranges a blanket round her.
Orin enters.

Orin Mum?
God, she doesn't know me.

Haydn She knows you.

Orin I have her to thank in a way. Berenice took me back after what happened.

Haydn Good for you. Must be nice to have a wife.

Orin A trial. Have to be sober. Felt sorry for me. Or the kids. I'm ashamed of what we did. I dream about it.

Haydn We had to stop her. Of course we did.

Orin She didn't want us to stop her. Why did you make me stop her? Maybe she had the right. I didn't fall asleep.

Haydn No?

Orin She took me by the arms. She looked me in the face.

Haydn What did she say?

Orin She – nothing. I couldn't say anything. She stroked the side of my face and I felt tears – I felt like a child, when I was a child. She always told me I was beautiful. When I was a kid.

Haydn Did she? She never said that to me.

Orin When I got into her bed in the mornings and the sun fell on the Indian bedspread which was red and turned the walls pink. This glow was everywhere. I was like a prince in a fairy tale. I didn't like school. She'd let me stay.

Haydn She should have encouraged you to go.

Orin (*quoting her*) 'School stamps the spirit out of you.'

Haydn I had to go.

Orin And whatever happened to me in the day. If I got pushed over at playtime I waited for her in the school playground to take me home. Seeing her face I felt everything bad fall away.

Haydn She spoilt you, Orin. That's why you can't stand on your own two feet.

Orin There's no need to be mean about it.

Haydn It's why you fail at everything. If you hadn't let her go in the first place she wouldn't be in this state.

Orin I know that. That's why I'm here. To make it up to her. I'll stay as long as I'm needed. You'd like that, wouldn't you, Mum?

He goes over to her.

Berenice thinks it's a good idea too. She doesn't want me back full time. Wants me to ease my way back in. I could live here part of the week then go back to the family at weekends. It's a perfect solution.

Haydn She can wrap you round her little finger.

Orin Berenice?

Haydn Her too.

Orin It wasn't easy for Mum when we were sent away. She told me that. You stayed away longer. Maybe that's why me and Mum were so close.

Haydn Every time Berenice kicks you out you come back to Mum with your tail between your legs. It's easier for me if you're not here. She pits us against each other. It drives me up the wall.

Orin Right. So you're saying –

Haydn I don't need you here. You can visit.

Orin I think I should stay.

Haydn Do you know what Freud said about mothers and sons?

Orin Something awful, was it?

Haydn You were her penis.

Orin God. How does he work that out? He was a maniac. Saying stuff like that. Just awful. Do you think she heard? It's embarrassing.

Haydn So it's more of a struggle to let the son go. That's why sons need fathers as role models, to help them cut the maternal tie. Go back to Berenice. Grow some balls. I would.

Orin Will you cope?

Haydn I've been coping till now.

Orin It's just – you don't like her.

Haydn I'm looking after her, aren't I?

Orin Berenice will be surprised to see me back. I was quite looking forward to a bit of distance. If I'm honest.

Haydn Fathers should be with their kids. Go on.

Orin Bye, Mum.

Virgie holds on to him. He frees himself. He exits. Tom enters.

Tom (*to Haydn*) You take a break.

She shakes her head. Watches as Tom begins reading to Virgie. He reads all the parts.

Where were we? Ah yes. Murder. My favourite bit.

(*As Clytemnestra.*) Help! Death is upon us! Is there no one to help?

(*Electra.*) There it is. Do you hear, do you hear?

(*Chorus.*) O what terrible cries!

(*Clytemnestra.*) Have mercy, my son, have mercy on your mother!

(*Electra, shouting through closed doors.*) You had none for him, nor his father before him.

(*Chorus.*) Now may the house and kingdom cry
  This is the end, the end of days of affliction.

(*As himself.*) I love the bloody chorus. You've got to give it to them.

(*Clytemnestra.*) Ah!

(*Electra.*) Strike her again, strike!

(*As himself.*) She's a baggage, that Electra.

(*Clytemnestra.*) Ah!

He makes this last cry fairly gruesome.
Sonia enters.

Sonia Do you think you should be reading her that?

Tom She can't get enough of it.

Sonia Couldn't you find something more cheerful?

Tom More cheerful than tragedy? I don't think so. Gets the pulse racing.

Sonia She doesn't need to get her pulse racing, she's had a stroke.

Tom You love it, don't you, Virgie? Yes, she does, she loves it. All the horror. Cleansing. Life-affirming.

Sonia I'm not sure you qualify as an appropriate adult. You haven't used a wardrobe in years. You just throw things on the floor like a toddler. I haven't been able to walk in a straight line in our bedroom for years.

Tom Such an effort putting clothes on hangers and then taking them off again. Life's too short. Virgie understands.

Sonia I think we have to go home today, Haydn.

Haydn Why?

Sonia We can't just live here. We have commitments. I'm incubating the arc of a novel.

Tom This is a good experience for me. In case I ever do a Holby.

Sonia You'll only get on as a corpse.

Tom Sensitive, isn't she, Virgie?

Sonia Sensitivity is overrated.

She exits.

Tom (*reads on*)
The curse has its way
The dead speak from the earth.
The tide is turned and the blood
Is sucked from the slayer
By the slain of long ago.
Here they come. Their hands are red
With the blood of sacrifice. And who condemns?
Not I.

Haydn lights up, indicates cigarette.

Haydn I ought to stop this. Apparently it's a nipple substitute.

Tom Can I have one?

Haydn We start off like that. Dependent. Powerless. And that's how we end up. The bit in between is – this.

Tom I think we probably will be heading back.

Haydn The haul I did at Sainsbury's. She won't be eating it.

Tom Sonia's pretty set on leaving.

Haydn Yes, but when have you ever listened to Sonia? I was thirteen.

Tom Thirteen.

Haydn Forty-five years ago.

Tom Preposterous. Time is.

Haydn When you moved in.

Tom The Republic of South Camden. Tenants' rights. I was just setting out It was the 1970s. That's really when the 1960s started. 1971. In Camden.

Haydn I thought you looked like Omar Sharif.

Tom I'm warming to this topic.

Haydn In *Doctor Zhivago*. I had that bandage over one half of my glasses.

Tom Oh yes.

Haydn It was a corrective thing. You called me the pirate.

Tom Sorry.

Haydn I didn't mind. Hideous. I was.

Tom No, no.

Haydn Virgie insisted on painting something pretty on my patch: a cactus. So I'm just saying I appreciated it. What you did. Pretending to flirt with me. Because there was no one else. To give me a sense that I was – female.

Tom Well, good, good. Was I flirting? I mean, was I good at it?

Sonia (*calling*) Can you come and take a look at this banana?

Haydn I wore those glasses for years because you said you liked them. When I finally got to the optician, she said, 'They were only a temporary thing. You should have replaced those years ago.' So you don't remember? I wondered if you did?

Tom Remember?

Haydn You gave me my first kiss.

Tom Did I? I was a bit of a cunt, wasn't I? Listen, look, I ought to get my act together. I'll strip the bed – don't worry on that account – unless Sonia's already . . . Yes I imagine she's done that.

Shirley enters with Sonia.

Shirley Let me have a look at her.
(*To Virgie.*) It's me, Shirley.
I'm taking an executive decision. This can't carry on.

Haydn How do you know? You've only just arrived.

Shirley I was a headmistress. I'm used to controlling situations I know very little about. It's an instinct. She needs to be in a home. You can pay me back when you sell up here.

Sonia I think Haydn is just anxious to see Virgie on her feet before any decisions are made.

Shirley On her feet? She's a vegetable. Sorry, Virgie, but you can't understand.

Tom You speak as to some thoughtless woman; you are wrong, my pulse beats firm.

Sonia Piss off, Tom. He's quoting.

Tom Neither of us are here, Virgie.

Shirley You don't want to be dragged into a life as a full-time carer, Haydn. Your life's been enough of a disappointment.

Haydn Virgie will be happier here. Surrounded by her work. She'll get better.

Shirley You mustn't blame yourself for this. Virgie started it.

Sonia We had some terrible experiences with Tom's mother.

Tom Poor old Mum.

Sonia She was an administrator for the NHS. I found her sitting after her bath naked, wet, shivering in a chair, no one had dried her. It was like she'd ended her life in a camp. What are we doing? Don't we even think for a moment that's going to be us?

Haydn I don't want her to suffer.

Sonia I've decided to start Zumba.

Shirley Talking of suffering.

Sonia Cuban, aerobic hybrid exercise. I can't even reach the top shelf at the supermarket, when I wake up in the morning I'm so stiff. What is that? Like life leaks out of you at night. We have to keep ourselves in good nick. Virgie's a warning. I've also embarked on West African drumming.

Shirley Yes, Virgie, thanks to you I've had a lot more sex. It got tricky for me when I got one breast.

Tom I'm sure the other breast is splendid,.

Shirley I haven't really thought about it.

Tom It wouldn't put me off. I've got athlete's foot.

Sonia That's not bloody comparable.

Tom A bald patch, flaky nails and man boobs. I'm hardly a great catch myself.

Sonia And you're married to me. Not that that's ever stopped you.

Shirley I don't want to have sex with you, Tom, I'm in the House of Lords.

Tom No, no, no, of course not, you must think it's awfully big-headed of me.

Shirley After what happened to Virgie I've started to feel bloody randy.

Sonia Tom had this affair.

Tom It gets very boring in Stratford. There's only one pub. The Dirty Duck's practically a knocking shop for thespians.

Sonia That's his excuse for shagging Caesar's wife.

Tom A two-year stint. Those Roman women knew how to dress.

Sonia throws her drink in Tom's face.

Sonia I don't know why we don't all do it.

Shirley What?

Sonia Kill ourselves like Virgie tried to. Aren't we just clinging on to our bit of unhappiness, forced to get up and go through it all – day after day . . . What is it we're living for? What have we done? Eaten, slept, tried to avoid unnecessary suffering.

Tom We are married.

Shirley I blame Virgie for this, she's forced us to become introspective.

Sonia I blame her a bit for me and Tom. She kept on sleeping with him and then I slept with her to even things up.
That'll give you something to think about.

She exits.

Shirley Too much information. Now my car is picking me up at three. You need to have come to a decision about Virgie by then. One thing I will say for Virgie, she had a lovely garden. I think I'll take a little stroll in it.

She exits.
Tom is left with Haydn.

Haydn I didn't know.

Tom What, Virgie and Sonia? Well, Virgie's always been a free spirit. Good for her.

Haydn No, Virgie and you.

He exits.
Haydn begins to feed Virgie.
Virgie spits out the food that Haydn is feeding her.
Haydn wipes Virgie's face in the food as punishment.
An aggressive act.
She goes and gets a cloth, wipes it clean.

Virgie Hay-dn.

Haydn There's a place, 'Lark House'. It has a jacuzzi. I'd love a jacuzzi. I can't be expected to – live here. Lark House, then.

Virgie with one mighty effort tries to hit out at her daughter, fails.

It's Lark House I worry about.

SCENE SIX

Haydn and Roy. Virgie's home. Six months later.

Roy Your mother, is she . . .?

Haydn What?

Roy – unusual?

Haydn She feels like she's been exiled.

Roy The language. For a lady her age. I've never been called an antediluvian twat.

Haydn This is her first visit home. A treat. Can you wait?

Roy Wait?

Haydn Hang around. I'm not sure she's going to last the lunch without an argument.

Roy I've got a pick-up at 1.15. Manningtree to Ipswich. One of my regulars.

Haydn Thirty quid.

Roy I'll call the base.

Haydn Thank you. What's your name?

Roy Roy.

Haydn Roy. From the Latin root *rex*, for king.

Roy I drive a Vauxhall Vectra.

Haydn You'll be beneficial too – a neutral presence.

Roy I thought you just wanted a minicab?

Haydn I want you to drive her back at a moment's notice. I'm not sure how she's going to react. Last year – she tried to drown herself.

Roy That's heavy.

Haydn I'm grateful to you for helping me out. I've always found Norfolk Cars extremely reliable.

Roy So, your mother . . .

Haydn We always call her Virgie, she didn't want to be known as 'Mother'. She was resistant to the role.

Roy I had planned a quiet afternoon. I picked you up once before. After you'd visited.

Haydn Did you?

Roy You were quite – agitated. I think she'd tried to bite you.

Sonia enters. She stops, sees Roy.

Haydn I've asked Roy to hang on. In case of an emergency exit.

Sonia Could be any one of us fleeing, Roy.

Virgie enters. She just about manages with a stick. It is hard going. She is physically frail but her mind is sharp.

Virgie Breadsticks?

Sonia I didn't know breadsticks were on the menu.

Virgie They're supposed to be there.

Sonia I don't like them because they're not what they say they are, more like a biscuit.

Virgie Well, I'm disappointed. Soak up the alcohol. We'll be pissed as mattresses before we get to the grub.

Haydn How did you sleep?

Virgie I don't sleep any more. Sleep's a thing of the past. Something I long for, something that's not coming back. You don't know what I'd do for a good night's kip. How did you sleep?

Haydn Fine.

Virgie Well, good for you. Is it too early for a drink?

Sonia Eleven fifty-five . . .

Virgie Mine's a rum and Coke.

Sonia Haven't done the ice yet.

She exits.

Haydn Welcome home, Virgie.

Virgie spots Roy.

Virgie Who are you? Do I know you?

Roy I just drove you. Your daughter asked me to hang on.

Virgie Hang on? But who are you?

Roy My name's Roy.

Virgie Is my daughter fucking you?

Roy I drive a taxi.

Virgie I repeat the question.

Haydn No, Mother. We are not having sexual relations.

Virgie No, you wouldn't have the style. Still, it is my first visit home – why would you bring a stranger to such an intimate occasion. I don't think it's an outlandish suggestion.

Haydn I asked Roy to stay. You might suddenly want to go.

Virgie I wanted to go for good, Roy, only my children wouldn't let me.

Haydn We're going to have lovely lunch.

Virgie It's only what you'd like to do to me but you can't accept it. That's why you stopped me.

Haydn Well, you've tried your best to drive me to it.

Roy Anyway, it's been nice meeting you all. I hope you have a good day and nothing untoward occurs.

Haydn You'd agreed to stay!

Roy I don't think this lady likes me.

Virgie Oh come on, Roy, you might as well stay now you're here – have a drink. I insist. (*Calls.*) Open some champagne, Tom. (*To Roy.*) It'll be good stuff, Roy, they're assuaging their guilt.

Roy I'm driving.

Virgie For Christ's sake. Fucking have some. Live, taste, enjoy. You're dead an eternity. Take it from me – I'm very attuned to it because I'm a suicidal octogenarian.

Roy Just the one.

Virgie Fabulous.

Haydn He's staying because of me.

Virgie Everything's about you.

Haydn He's being compassionate. He sees I'm in difficulty and he wants to help me. Thank you, Roy, I acknowledge your gesture.

Virgie He couldn't wait to get out of the front door two minutes ago. It was only because I offered him vintage champagne that he changed his mind.

Haydn Don't twist the truth.

Virgie Well then, Roy. You could clear this up for us once and for all. And right in the nick of time. You can offer what the Greeks called *nous*. An objective healing truth to lay all the old ghosts.

All look at Roy.

Roy Oh dear. Well, it's a bit of both, really. If I'm honest.

Virgie Oh but darling Roy, you're not honest. Very few of us are. And we get into the habit of lying most of all to ourselves and then we're lost. Yes, lost. And there

I gave you a chance and you stalled at the fence. Never mind. You're in company.

Sonia has entered.

Sonia How is life in the – in your new accommodation?

Virgie Like being dead without the alleviating condition of insensibility. Be you in a few years.

Sonia Quite a few.

Virgie Goes fast though. The more behind you the more it speeds up, rushing you to obscurity and incontinence pads.

Sonia Live in the present. That's what I say.

Virgie I've shrunk an inch since Friday. My hearing aid makes weird noises. Am I underwater? We're being inebriated by constant television. Martin Clunes visits the lemurs of Madagascar.

Tom enters with drinks.

Sonia Oh Tom, thank God.

Tom Hello, Virgie, how wonderful.

Virgie What?

Tom To see you looking so . . . yourself.

Virgie Don't patronise me, Tom, I'm not a moron. I just look like a moron because my neck is bad.

Tom You've never lost your sense of humour, Virgie. That's wonderful too.

Virgie What's wrong with him? Is it senility?

Sonia Then you could join Virgie at Lark House, Tom.

Haydn The home's lovely and they have vegetarian options.

Virgie Also known as the omelette.

Shirley enters from garden.

Shirley Spectacular – the colours, those lovely little blue flowers. Who wouldn't want to live for ever?

Virgie Me, but you bastards fucked it up.

Shirley Happy homecoming for the day, darling.

She spots Roy.

So who's this?

Virgie Haydn's bit of squeeze.

Shirley (*to Roy*) I'm the aunt. How have you ended up in this madhouse?

Roy I don't know. All families are a bit mad, aren't they?

Virgie Oh Roy, you almost verged on the interesting.

Shirley So is this your new man?

Haydn You're getting the wrong end of the stick.

Sonia He drives a cab.

Shirley That's how they met? Oh, that's darling.

Tom Is anyone else finding this excruciating?

Sonia He picks her up from the station when she gets the train down.

Shirley Of course and why not, with lovely Roy waiting in his warm cab.

Virgie You're making it sound like porn, Shirley.

Shirley Really? That good.

Haydn I'm sorry about this, Roy. It's a collective fantasy.

Roy It's quite nice.

Virgie Roy, have you ever been to Venice?

Roy No.

Virgie Well everyone should go once in their lives. I want to give Roy my holiday in Venice. It was my birthday present last year.

Roy I don't feel I can.

Virgie Don't be such a self-sacrificing wimp.

Shirley Don't be offended, Roy. She's only doing it to annoy me. It was my present.

Virgie Thank you for imputing base motives to me, Shirley. It would just make me very happy to think of Roy on the Ponte dei Sospiri. Or seeing a Tintoretto at the Scuolo Grande di San Rocco: *The Crucifixion*. Tintoretto has Christ in really rather tremendous physical shape. Muscular pulsing arms and he's not afraid to suffer, Roy, because to be afraid to suffer is to be afraid to live. He is driving his tragedy forward to its inevitable end.

Haydn Don't patronise Roy, he's capable of arranging a city break.

Roy I picked a bloke up from Braintree once thought he was Buddha. He wasn't.

Virgie These things, Roy, these sights, are spiritually enriching. Shirley doesn't understand these things because she has the soul of a bureaucrat.

Shirley Not that again.

Virgie Now Roy. Say you're going to go on this wonderful trip to Venice –

Roy No, Virgie.

Haydn Thank you, Roy.

Virgie Piss off then.

Sonia Oh dear – Come on, let's get ourselves a nice plateful. Maybe that will cheer Virgie up?

Virgie Cheer me up? I'm suicidal. I can't bear pusillanimous platitudes. That's you all over, Sonia.

Sonia I'll get yours, Virgie.

Virgie I can get my own grub. I'm not dead yet.

Sonia Lovely. Lovely. Here we go.

They all exit.
Haydn left with Roy.

Haydn I know how it looks, to a stranger. Putting her in Lark House. It looks selfish.

Roy Not a total stranger.

Pause.

When you were upset that time we had that drink when I dropped you off. Nice wine: Merlot.

Haydn Right.

Roy Second bottle was a Sauvignon.

Haydn Second bottle?

Roy You've forgotten.

Haydn The details.

Roy Its existence.

Haydn No, I knew I remembered your face.

Roy Flattery. Just before Christmas it was.

Haydn I'd just put Virgie 'away'. She was acting out.

Roy Then we hit the Limoncello. I had to get a cab home. I was the laughing stock of the office.

Haydn Do you remember what we talked about?

Roy You said something about that night – the one you thought she drowned but she came back.

Haydn What did I say?

Roy Really you wished she – she had died.

Haydn I've got guts when I'm pissed.

Roy By the third bottle that is what we all want, isn't it? Someone dead or alive? Or sex.

Haydn Anything else? Apart from matricide?

Roy Don't beat yourself up.

Haydn You'll be having some lunch? It's a buffet.

Pause.

Were we intimate?

Roy What? Well –

Haydn Because I apologise.

Roy Don't apologise.

Haydn I don't think there could be anything sustained between us.

Roy Oh yes. Yes. Yes. I knew that.

Haydn I was just reiterating it for the sake of clarity.

Roy It was a nice evening. Is it because of my job?

Haydn No. Well, yes.

Roy I'm just glad it's not because I've got a small knob.

Haydn I don't remember thinking that.

Roy That's good because I've never had any complaints you know. I'm not boasting. I'm not saying it's outstanding.

Haydn I'm sure I wouldn't be fussy in that department.

Roy Why not?

Haydn That's just not me.

Roy Because when I got your call about today, well, I did wonder. If, you know – you were up for round two.

Haydn I'm not.

Roy Well, I know that now.
You said you'd done something. You said you weren't a good person. I said I thought you were quite nice and I'd be interested in getting to know you better.

Haydn I think I probably did you a favour.

Roy Why?

Haydn I haven't proved to be relationship material. Not everybody is. I know our society is obsessed with couples. Awkward for those of us that don't fit that box.

Roy I wasn't talking about marriage. Just the odd drink. Maybe a weekend in the Isle of Wight. My brother lives there.

Haydn Well, that's very sweet.

Roy So you never wanted kids.

Haydn No.

Roy I thought most women did.

Haydn Apparently not. Not everyone's cut out for that. Have you met my mother?

Roy I can talk to you.

Haydn Right.

Roy We've just actually had a proper talk. I value that. So maybe you should reconsider.

Haydn Reconsider?

Roy Having a drink with me sometime. Haydn.

One by one the others gather with lunch. It's not round a table, a buffet affair.

Virgie Let's make small talk. Shirley's in politics. Any more wars on the horizon?

Shirley I'm loving the veg. Are you, Roy?

Virgie I was larking around with the residents of Lark House the other day. With Honour who thinks the nurses are Nazis and Geoffrey who is mostly trying to wank himself off but not succeeding. I often nod off to his heartrending cries of lamentation at his defunct organ. Anyway I was chatting the breeze to them as you do, about how we could be useful citizens in this time of economic catastrophe. I think they should send old people to war – Citizens of the Third Age. We'd jump at it; free travel to exotic places; no heating bills; we could while away the time between target practice playing bridge; stepping on a land mine, quicker than cancer. No one would really mind. Eighty years. Shot by insurgents in Kabul while winching her mate's wheelchair out of quicksand. Saves the NHS loads: the answer to austerity. No wasted life. No bereft mothers weeping at Wootton Bassett, our mas are long dead. No wobbly kiddie-writing saying 'Daddy we miss you' – our kids have grown up and hate our guts. It's a solution.

Tom Dad's army. Quite funny.

Sonia People couldn't bear to look at pensioners all shot up.

Virgie They smell of wee, they're as deaf as posts and they're so fucking horribly jolly. They know no one's going put up with them unless they're humiliatingly upbeat. Christ. I'd actually enjoy shooting them.

Sonia This is a bit dark.

Virgie Yes. Anyway – where do I sign?

Sonia I don't think you should attack Shirley, she's had cancer.

Shirley Yes, and it's fucking come back. Be a bloody irony if Virgie outlives me.

Virgie You should have thought of that before you press-ganged me into existence.

Sonia I'm so sorry to hear – Shirley.

Shirley I don't want to talk about it.

Sonia Lots of people survive cancer, Shirley. You should try hemlock root.

Virgie Sounds poisonous, maybe I should try it.

Sonia How's the hummus, Roy?

Roy Very nice, thank you.

Virgie Is your mother coming, Roy?

Roy No.

Virgie Dead, is she?

Roy Yes.

Virgie Lucky cow. No point in asking her then.

Tom No. Bit tasteless.

Virgie So Roy, what's your position on euthanasia?

Sonia Top up, Roy.

Roy I'm fine. Thank you.

Shirley We don't know anything about Roy yet.

Tom What would we talk about if Roy wasn't here?

Virgie You'd have to talk to me. Acknowledge my wretched existence. I'm like Banquo at the banquet. Embarrassing.

Tom

'Which of you have done this?
Thou canst not say I did it. Never shake
Thy gory locks at me.'

Haydn Tom's an actor.

Roy In anything at the moment, Tom?

Tom *Lear*. I'm Gloucester – I had this moment the other night on stage listening to the others – and then no one was speaking, silence fell and I thought some bugger's forgotten their lines and then I realised it was me and I could see Kent looking at me thinking any moment now the lines will pop out of his mouth and the whole machine will trundle on – but he could have waited an eternity because my head was empty as a bubble.

Shirley What happened?

Tom I said something. Not something Shakespeare had written, mind you. Something about a herring.

Roy That sounds Shakespearean.

Sonia That's getting older, Tom. Soon all the Viagra in the world won't give you an erection. Then what will you do?

Tom I'll write memoirs. Get lost in that.

Virgie Why do you always want to be lost, Tom?

Tom What happens after you're found? That's the bit that scares me.

Sonia Are you married, Roy?

Tom How could he be if he's seeing Haydn?

Roy I'm not seeing her.

Shirley Bread, Roy?

Haydn I'm sorry about this.

Roy I'm okay.

Shirley What's your family like, Roy?

Roy I've got an uncle who plays the ukulele.

Tom Not up there with the house of Atreus.

Orin enters.
General exclamation.

Orin Sorry, sorry. I thought we said two.

Sonia Make a place for Orin.

Orin Hello, Mother.

Virgie Why do you want to get involved with this family, Roy? Has anybody told him? I have time to think while I'm rotting in my present institution. Why don't my children love me?

Haydn Mum. She's impossible.

Virgie I blame the books they learnt to read with. Daddy at the office. Mummy looking out of the window while she's washing up. I should have burnt them. I was an artist I wanted to paint what I saw out of the window. *Kirche, Kinder, Küche* – that was what Adolf Hitler had in mind for women and that's who my children sided with.

Haydn We did not side with Adolf Hitler.

Shirley They weren't even born.

Virgie In order to paint, you have to live and to live, to be frank with you, Roy, you have to fuck –

Shirley More showing off.

Tom It's honest.

Virgie I tried to do both as much as possible but domesticity suffocated me. It's a hard world for a woman who really wants to live, most of them end up neurotic like Sonia or power-crazed like Shirley or repressed and vengeful like my daughter.

Sonia Don't paint us in a good light just for Roy's sake.

Roy I meet all sorts driving a cab.

Virgie Just once I went AWOL, Roy. The Capodimonte, Naples. *Judith Slaying Holofernes*. Anyone know it? Artemisia Gentileschi. Once falsely ascribed to Caravaggio. They'd missed her signature. I was gripped by an overwhelming desire to see it. I stood in front of the canvas, could see the strokes of her brush. I soaked it in. The bloody bedroom scene; the horror of the deed; Holofernes the victim. His head, close to us, flooded with light, forced down by Judith who drives the sword home through his neck, a splattering of blood at her wrists. In an act of extreme audacity and daring Artemisia used the man who raped her as the model for the general – her own face for Judith, the avenger. She put all her rage, her sense of injustice into the paint, with her talent she took on the world and through that she was I think, liberated

Roy That sounds very dynamic.

Virgie You're a better man than my ex-husband, Roy.

Roy Thank you.

Haydn Mum.

Virgie Haydn's never forgiven me for her father. She's hunched over that like a squirrel over the last nut in the universe. He'd come in front of my paintings.

Orin Oh God, do we have to hear this story? It's chewing up my balls.

Virgie Stood in front of them, face clouded over because they scared him and he used to say to me, 'What are the kids having for tea?' and I'd say, 'You sort it out – I'm working,' and he'd say 'That's your department' – my department? – and I said to him, 'You're killing me, that's what you're trying to do' – kill me – I left him. Who wouldn't, who wanted to live?

Haydn The thing is, Virgie, we didn't want to leave him, he didn't want to leave.

Virgie Yes, well, that's history and if you want to be weighed down by history go ahead.

Haydn Really, after that he was a very sad man, lost without his kids and you.

Virgie He wasn't that sad – he went to Australia and married an art collector who specialised in dots.

Shirley Dots, was it?

Sonia Shall we toast?

Tom God yes. Sitting here without alcohol. Are we mad?

He tops them up.

Sonia Well, let's toast Virgie. Let's hope, Virgie, that you get to – what's the word I'm looking for, Tom?

Tom I've no idea.

Sonia Well, everyone knows what I mean.

Tom The novelist strikes back.

They all raise their glasses: cheers.

Here's to Virgie. And to Roy.

Orin Who the hell is he?

Virgie He drives a minicab. He's shagging Haydn.

Roy Hello.

Haydn No, he's not.

Tom Virgie, it's great to see you back in the bosom of your friends and family. May you long remain.

Virgie Where are my paintings?

Sonia Did you take them down? Haydn?

Virgie Orin – get one of my paintings.

Haydn They were very loud.

Virgie I demand to see them.

Haydn They're safe. They're all in the spare bedroom.

Virgie begins to take off her clothes.

Sonia What are you doing, Virgie?

Virgie I'm not ashamed.

Shirley Oh God, she's taking her clothes off.

Virgie I want to see my work.

Haydn Stop making an exhibition of yourself.

Shirley No one wants to see your bush, Virgie. Especially Roy.

Roy That's very considerate.

Virgie This is a protest.

Haydn Get a painting, Orin.

Orin What one do you want?

Haydn Any. Go on.

Virgie Use your initiative.

Orin goes.

Sonia Put your blouse back on.

Sonia helps Virgie put her blouse back on.

Virgie (*to Roy*) I'm going to show you one of my paintings. Roy.

Orin enters with one.

There. Roy, so what do you think of that?

Roy It's really – nice. It's not – well I don't know what it is, but it's emotional. Isn't it?

Virgie Yes, Roy, it is. This is my life Roy – not the people around me. This. What Haydn didn't mention, Roy, was that when I left them alone to have my artistic epiphany they were kids: Haydn was eleven, Orin was six and Helen was three. As a result of that my children were taken away. I got them back – not Helen. Not the youngest, of course. So these things have to be weighed up. What do you think of the painting now, Roy? Do you still like it as much? Is the blue still that special blue?

Haydn All through our childhood there was this little ghost. Of our sister who we never saw again.

Shirley Yes, we don't usually talk about that, Roy.

Virgie Blame me.

Haydn I do blame you. You were unnatural.

Virgie Yes. I was. Good for me. Fuck nature. Because when you look at the great masters, Roy, how do you judge them? Do you look at a Caravaggio and think murderer, or a Picasso and say thief, Schiele pornographer? Do you revere Banksy less because he's defiling municipal buildings? No, you celebrate them because they've lived bigger lives than you do so they could give you what you need.

Roy Yes.

Haydn I think it's time to go now, Virgie.

Virgie And if you blame me it's because in your heart of hearts you know you've never lived and I have. You're mediocrities and you envy me.

Tom Oh God, Virgie, is that what you think of us?

Sonia Yes it is.

Virgie My daughter is the worst. She knew I was coming back. She was old enough. She could have managed. I left them bread and cheese. She waited till I'd gone and she walked over the road to the interfering bitch – there was a perfectly nice old girl next door – she would never have interfered. And that's how I lost my youngest child. I was punished. Revenge, jealousy. The last resort of the talentless. Because, Roy . . .

Her words are breaking up. This begins to alarm everyone.

I was a female Prometheus – eaten from the inside by a raging insistence – if you feel colour like I – did – not a matter of elegance or prettiness – it's a god wrenching itself through the ends of my fingers –

She points to the painting.

Do you see – do you see –

Haydn You'd better take her home now, Roy.

Virgie sits.

Virgie I'm not going anywhere.
My daughter.

Virgie dies sitting up.

Haydn I should never have been put in that position. I was eleven. Perhaps you should consider that?

Roy Is it time now?

SCENE SEVEN

Ten days later. Miranda, twenty-eight, stands in the room. Late afternoon.

Miranda Am I the last?

Tom The last?

Miranda Well, not family.
I don't want to miss my train.

Tom We're driving back, you could come with us.

Miranda Really?

Tom No problem.

Miranda Wonderful. I'm sorry, I'm quite vocal. When I cry.

Tom Yes. That's a good thing.

Miranda I've always been a very loud crier. It was noted in my family. I'm not very good at holding back.

Tom Ah. Well, that's no bad thing.

Miranda I'm impulsive as well. I came here on impulse but I adored Virgie and I had to come.

Tom I think you cried louder than anyone.

Miranda And I never bring tissues. So thank you for –

Tom Please. I was overflowing.

Miranda I still feel really sad.

Tom That might be the cava.

Miranda Hug me.

They hug.
He does. Sonia walks in. She sees this and walks out.

Tom That was my wife.

Miranda She seems nice.

Tom So Virgie taught you, you were saying –

Miranda When I was a student, yes.

Haydn enters.

Tom Haydn, did you meet –

Miranda Miranda.

Tom Earlier?

Haydn No.

Miranda I was the loud sobbing.

Haydn Yes, you were.

Tom Never out of place at a funeral. Virgie taught her.

Haydn To cry?

Miranda At the Royal College of Art. I was a great admirer of your mother's work.

Haydn Why?

Miranda ?

Pause.

It must have been isolating for her living down here.

Haydn She liked it.

Miranda She couldn't afford London, that's why she moved, she told me. Even though her work sold it wasn't enough, you know.

Haydn She always got by.

Miranda I've got one of her paintings. *Glad Ocean.* I look at it every day and it makes me happy.

Tom Well, what an affirmation.

Miranda She made it by throwing paint at the canvas. Then she rolled in it.

Haydn Yes, that sounds like her.

Miranda She allowed herself to be influenced by the American abstract expressionists in the fifties. She adapted their energy to an open and joyous lyricism. She was a superlative colourist.

Haydn Are you planning on staying the night? Because if you want to catch the last train . . .

Miranda No. Tom is driving me home.

Haydn I'm not sure Sonia is going to agree to that.

Tom Really. Shit.

Haydn She's just broken another glass. She's supposed to be washing up.

Tom It's all a misunderstanding.

Sonia enters.

Sonia I've cut my hand. That's your fault.

Tom For fuck's sake, Sonia, how did you do that?

Sonia I was washing up. I hate death. My mother used to say you'll be so tired when you're old you won't mind dying. That was a lie.

Tom She had to say something.

Sonia Don't think I haven't got your number.

Miranda What?

Sonia I have a slut radar.

Tom Sonia.

Miranda I wouldn't sleep with your husband, he's too old.

Tom See, Sonia? I'm decrepit.

Miranda Do I still get a lift?

Tom You'll get a lift. Miranda was taught by Virgie.

Sonia Oh, how wonderful.

Miranda I used to go for coffee with her. I loved that. Felt like being singled out. But we both had the thing of coping with depression.

Haydn Virgie was never depressed.

Miranda We both started Hatha yoga, that helped. She told me it wasn't easy being a female artist in the fifties – or an abstractionist – the two together – men made their names and she always snuck in on the sidelines. I think she came down here in a kind of defeat.

Sonia She exhibited at the Biennale.

Haydn She won prizes, second prize at the John Moores exhibition.

Tom She had a one-woman show in New York.

Miranda She never got what she deserved.

Haydn You've made a particular study of my mother.

Miranda She was always growing, her work was – once she had an architect lover, from him she learnt the value of geometric shapes.

Tom While having a shag. Marvellous economy.

Miranda Her paintings manifested her ongoing fascination for non-representative organic forms.

Haydn I'd really like it if you left now. I've had a tiring day, I buried my mother.

Shirley enters.

Shirley I was just thinking we ought to have a memorial to Virgie.

Sonia A bench – some people have a bench.

Miranda Her work is her memorial. You should think about a retrospective.

Orin enters with Shirley.

Orin Did I miss it?

Haydn Yes.

Orin My own mother's funeral.

Shirley Yes.

Orin Christ.

Tom Least it wasn't yours. Unforgivable to be late for that.

Shirley She'd understand. She was late all the time.

Orin Sat-nav – fucking useless – too upset to follow it. Did the kids get here?

Sonia They've gone back on the train.

Orin Their mother.

Sonia Her too.

Orin Well that's – just – not going to impress them. We're on another break.

Tom Lovely girls.

Sonia Spare us. This is Miranda. A student of Virgie's.

Miranda Would you like a drink?

Orin I would, but I'm an alcoholic.

Sonia We're thinking of a bench for Virgie.

Shirley God spare me from a fucking bench. I don't want an endless series of arses parked on my bit of eternity.

Sonia You aren't going anywhere yet.

Shirley Not if I can help it.

Orin Have we met before?

Miranda Are you a waiter?

Orin No.

Miranda Then we haven't.

Orin You could be –

Haydn Who?

Orin No one. Helen. Like Helen.

Miranda Helen?

Haydn She's too young for Helen. She'd be fifty-one.

Orin And dead of course.

Miranda I'm definitely not her.

Orin Well, we say dead. Not really dead. Just lost to us. So metaphorically dead.

Miranda I'm twenty-eight. And I should be going.

Orin We all got put into care, but she was three so she never came back.

Miranda Poor Virgie.

Haydn It was her fault.

Miranda She told me all about it. She was punished. They took her child. For that.

Tom How will you get to the station?

Miranda I'll trust to the universe.

Orin Don't go.

Sonia Give her a lift, Tom. Or she won't make it.

Shirley I loved your speech, Tom.

Tom Thank you. 'Nothing left remarkable beneath the visiting moon.'

Sonia He did *Antony and Cleopatra*, Northampton, 2002.

Tom I'd do it better now. I think that about everything.

Shirley I'm going to hate resting.

Tom The point is doing things in the moment – the art of life – but there's no rehearsal. That's what's good about acting.

Sonia Except it's not real.

Miranda Can I take something? Small. A memento.

Haydn No. It'll muck up the probate.

Orin An ashtray?

Haydn Give her a lift, Tom.

Tom exits with Miranda.

Orin That was a bit –

Haydn We don't know who she is really.

Orin picks up something small, runs out after them.

Sonia Well, Tom can shag her now.

Shirley I don't think he'll shag her. He'll be driving like a cartoon or she'll miss the 6.03.

Sonia What do you think, Haydn, in your professional opinion?

Haydn Driving, I imagine.

Sonia Yes, I suppose. I always feel like I'm being cheated of something. Why is that?
You know what I fancy now? A bit of drumming.

Shirley Have you got a drum?

Sonia It travels with me.

She gets it.

Shirley She hasn't gone to get it, has she? Oh God, I think she has.

Sonia You try that – I'll use the table. You start off with a simple 3/2 rhythm.

Demonstrates.

Shirley Not at my age. I like my drums at a distance with lots of other instruments mixed in.

Sonia Once you try it you really get into it.

Shirley It's not some female empowerment nonsense, is it? That stuff churns my guts.

Sonia There is a joy of drumming with other women.

Shirley God spare me.

She tries.

Actually it's quite good fun.

They beat out a rhythm.

Have a go, Haydn. Just imagine you're hitting someone you don't like.

This builds up.

I'm actually feeling it in my fanny.

Sonia That's not unusual.

Shirley I'm really good at this.

Sonia Shout things if you like. It's therapeutic. We are women.

Shirley I'm not saying that nonsense.

Sonia Something else then.

Shirley Give me back my tit! Oh this is fun.

She starts to cry.

Now what's happening?

Sonia It's perfectly normal. Keep up the drumming.

Shirley is crying and drumming.

Shirley This is mega.

Haydn joins in. They dance round the room.

Haydn Virgie, I miss you, you murderer.

Orin enters. He is stunned by the drumming. They stop, laugh.

Shirley Well, today's done. We can draw a line under everything. Shall we sit out for a bit?

Orin Saw them off. Don't you always think, 'Is this Helen?' or is that . . .

Haydn She's probably a mother of three living in Hull.

Orin Sounds good.

Haydn If she wanted to get in touch she would have.

Orin She was three. She won't remember us. She'll be angry.

Haydn I'm sorry, Orin.

Tom re-enters.

Sonia Did you see her off?

Tom No, she suddenly remembered a friend nearby. She's gone for a visit.

Sonia Did you kiss her?

Tom You know me.

Sonia Did you?

Tom Yes. She's a good kisser.
Of course I fucking didn't. Just stop it, Sonia, will you? I'm a fucking philanderer but I must be near the end of the road.

Sonia Come and wave us off.

Haydn Do you still want the chest?

Sonia Will it fit? It seems a bit –

Haydn Take it. The place is up for sale Monday.

Sonia Tom's back. Gives him gyp.

Tom There's nothing left of me really that works.

Orin I'll give you a hand. Then I'll probably set off. I can't stand it here without Mum.

Shirley I'll open the doors.

Orin grabs the chest, staggers out.
Shirley and Orin exit.

Tom Well, look, good luck. So it's finished with you and that –

Haydn There was never anything with Roy.

Tom Bit dull. Bit young for you. Not like me.

Haydn Well, you're married. Everyone's got someone. Except me.

Tom I've got Sonia. It's not all roses.

Haydn kisses Tom.
Sonia enters.

Haydn Sorry, Sonia.

Sonia Nonsense, what for? I don't want to hear sorry. You've just buried your mother.

Tom Did they get the chest in?

Sonia They're tying it on with rope.

Tom That'll spill off on the motorway, then. That's life.

Sonia Goodbye.

They exit.
Shirley comes back in.

Shirley Just now, Haydn, just now, in the garden, I very sharply missed Virgie. I got a sense of her I'd never had in life. As if I could see her. As if she'd become clearer somehow now she was dead. The dead are more vivid than the living. Unfair.

She willed herself to die. She didn't think of me. She knew I was ill. I haven't got a choice.

Haydn Do you want to take some of the sandwiches back with you?

Shirley I always wondered why she didn't tell you.

Pause.

Because I always said to her – Haydn ought to know.

Haydn What?

Shirley When she was in Naples, when she ran away. She always said to me you were too young to really know what you were doing. And that you'd blame yourself for Helen being lost. But it wasn't your fault.

Haydn Then I got sent away to Aunt Hilda's for two years like she couldn't bear to see me.

Shirley You were young. You know. We have to forgive ourselves these things. What are you going to do with all the paintings?

The horn of the car beeps.

That's my car.
Virgie could have tried harder with Helen. Tried harder to get her back, in my opinion. But in some way it suited her – she could get on with her art. She was obsessed. Too driven. Will you be all right here tonight alone? Of course you will, you're Virgie's daughter.

She exits.
Noise of goodbyes outside.
Haydn comes back in alone. She is absolutely stricken.
She takes the paintings – we see her exit with them into the garden. She returns. we see her get matches and a can of petrol. She is about to exit when Miranda re-enters.

Miranda I came back to see if I could buy a painting from you.

Pause.

What are you doing? Are you going to burn them? You really can't do that.
That's murder. That's destroying her immortality.

Haydn I don't really like her paintings.

Miranda Let me talk you through one. Come outside with me now and let me tell you. Let me show you. How to look.

Haydn stares at Miranda.

End of play.